Visions Of Love - An Anthology Of Verse And Quote - Volume 1

written by Jane K Wilson and Steven Lloyd

Jane and Steve in 2011

If The Heavens Would Only Open

If the heavens would only open
and choirs of jubilant exalting angels
sung their exquisite religious requiems
Who among the denizens of earth
could ever again drop their cigarette end to the ground
or complain that their neighbour had taken their parking space?
Who could blow their car horn
and shout 'motherfucker' at the vagrant on the sidewalk?

I was reminded that the morning birdsong
is in fact in tune with the musical key of Father Sun.
It seems that the birds can readily hear
something that we humans can not.
The frequencies of Earth Mother are rising however.
And my feeling is that very soon
the postman shall be whistling 'Jerusalem' on his morning round
and that the love letters he delivers
will be wet with his exultant tears.

Steven Lloyd April 2011

You are like nobody else in the world. I am calm and peaceful just perfectly content, knowing you're the only one for me. I love you because the world is fooled by the smile on my face but you see the pain in my eyes and just help me soothe it. I love you because the world tells me that I'm pretty but you make me feel beautiful. I love you because the world views me as a lady but you make me simply feel like a woman and like a little girl at the same time. I love you because the world made me cynical but you made me believe in love again. I love you because the world is too cruel for me to share my secrets but you so easily allow me to disclose them to you. I love you because the world knows I'm strong enough to fight my battles but you stand there to fight alongside me anyway. All that matters is that you are here now with me and all I know is that I sure as hell hate it when you're not.

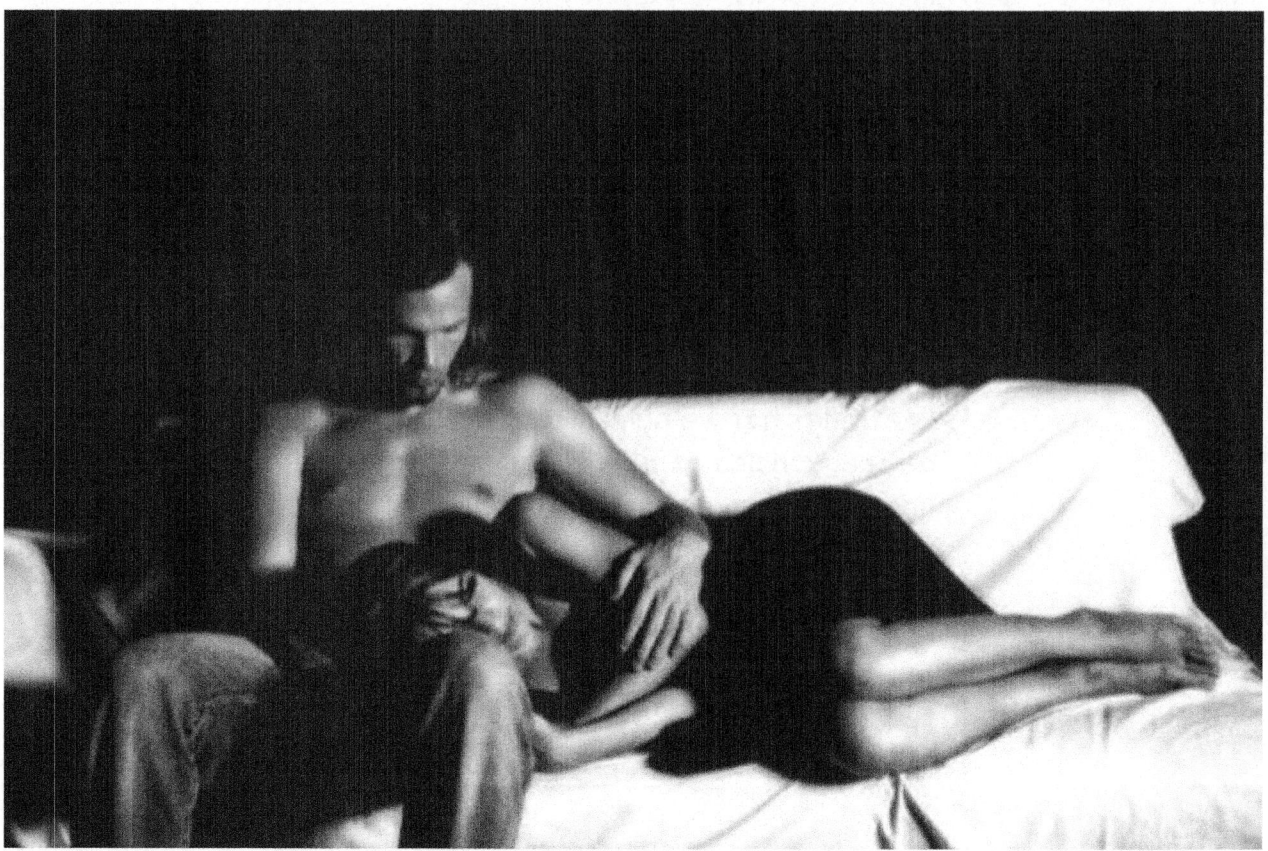

I'm tired, can't think of anything and want only to lay my face in your lap, feel your hand on my head and remain like that through all eternity. - Franz Kafka

I often find myself reliving the past memories of us. I think I'm just in love with the familiar feeling of loving you. I can't help it. I want you because I don't know how to not want you. I simply don't like not knowing how to do things but incidentally no one seems to have any helpful advice and just sometimes I wish I could just remove the want, extract it, but I get the feeling the want is not one of those things you can readily extract, like rotten teeth or slow-moving venom. The want is undulating somewhere in the ether. I often tell myself I shouldn't want you because you're not mine, and I can understand all the sensible and convincing reasons I shouldn't, but when it comes to the actual practice of not wanting you, something falls off that table of logic and splatters unceremoniously all over the floor.

I fell in love with the way you entered a room like both April and May - coming in out of the cold with the promise to grow flowers in the vacant places in my chest. - Lucy Quin

It's the end of April and more precisely the beginning of our story. I always wondered how could it be humanely possible to fall in love with someone in such a short amount of time. You are the person who has mended my broken heart by giving me yours. It's hard not to fall in love with someone when they see the mixed up parts of your soul and still love you. When they understand the darkest and dustiest corners of your mind when no one else could. Attraction is common. What is rare is having someone who wants to grow and build with you. A soul partner, a soul confidante, a soul mate. This kind of love and a passion like ours comes but once in a lifetime. Isn't it beautiful how someone can walk into our lives in the most unexpected way, perhaps even just in an insane manner and that's all it takes to be unable to imagine our entire lives without them.

There are millions of people in the world, and the spirits will see that most of them you never have to meet. But there are one or two you are tied to, and the spirits will cross you back and forth, threading so many knots until they catch and you finally get it right. - Jodi Picoult

So we all have a soulmate. Maybe platonically, or maybe not. But there's someone out there, and they're made for you, and I think that's beautiful. It was a day unlike any other because they loved each other, you see, but neither knew it of the other. Expectancy loomed, lingered, and danced in the air like a heavy fog awaiting a lover's whisper; an affirmation, a certain gentle presence in the foreground that could illuminate the veil of misunderstandings and misgivings. She waited, listening intently for it, but all the moment contained for her was a delicate hush which wasn't exactly the absence of sound, but the white noise of words left unsaid. 'I love you, I love you, I love you' their voices echoed inside one another's heart, as if they were trying to catch the caterpillar the second it flew off as a butterfly. Unattainable and unrepeatable. In any case and where feelings for her were omnipresent, the expression thereof alluded him. After all, it is not so much what we do to one another, in so far as what we do to ourselves. For who shall be saved if not to have first drowned? Such was the inconsistency of the heart. Its holes, its ravines, its majesty illuminating the darkness.

Sometimes when I look at you, I feel I'm gazing at a distant star. It's dazzling, but the light is from tens of thousands of years ago. Maybe the star doesn't even exist any more. Yet sometimes that light seems more real to me than anything. - Haruki Murakami

It is both comforting and torturous to know that I have never loved another soul like I love yours. We embraced the present through our melancholy the way the wings of doves needed, desired the air, unencumbered in the surrender and free to go any which way the wind were to blow. Could it be that flight was unwittingly only purposeful in finding the right branch to ultimately perch on? Does the weight of the soul not make the birds feathers at times feel like they're moving through quicksand, and only finding the sticky sap of a beautiful tree to melt one into the other and create a common thread tethering us to this beautiful world? And is this not the very thing that keeps us from floating up and away, lost in the endless ether? So fall into me my darling, as I fall deeper in love with you.

We must have one love, one great love in our life, since it gives us an alibi for all the moments when we are filled with despair. - Albert Camus

I saw him for the first time not knowing much about him, and I felt a pull of energy within my solar plexus. My mind began to grasp at something, a vague memory, a slight impression of something that felt familiar. There were no assurances, only the known twin souls of hope and desire catapulting us into fear and despair, and back and forth and back again, seemingly without end or beginning, just a deep perpetual longing spinning itself out to infinity inside some distant black hole. There was no escape or salvation, save for the mellifluous current of waves the moon waged against desolate banks with her tempestuous moods, luring me into the gulf of him.

Perhaps there is a language which is not made of words and everything in the world understands it. Perhaps there is a soul hidden in everything and it can always speak, without even making a sound, to another soul. - Frances Hodgson Burnett

He stood waiting patiently for her. Like a candle, she came flickering into the periphery. He could sense the impending doom of one who's about to lose their heart within the foreign land of another, and like an offering to the Gods, not knowing whether he'd be struck down in a wrath of lightning or knighted by Cupid's arrow, his fate was quite simply beyond his control. The sky was full of richly decadent clouds, the soft kind you wished to rest your head upon at night with dangerous surrender, that fill your dreams with amorous gusts and languid sighs. Anticipation, their constant companion, continued to gently dangle mercifully in the air. Then he stepped nearer to her. Her hair like snow, dancing in the wind. In that moment he wished he were paralyzed. Nothing could have been more agonizing or more beautiful than to forever prolong this moment of uncertainty. He kissed life into her trembling lips and breathed passion into her soul. He made her feel alive again. The waves, almost melancholic for them, seemed to whisper in a vague dissonance what their hearts could not reveal, 'He loves you, she loves you' each time the waves crashed upon the shore, the ocean licking their feet. This is only the continuation of a story that began long ago, in an age before time invented clocks and a life was instead measured by the beatings of the heart. Once upon a time there was a girl who followed the sun and a boy who followed the moon and they were forever linked in longing. Two wholes which made up a half universe, unable to conceive the entire thing because they were always together, yet forever apart. This is their story. The story of how the sun desired the moon and fell into the ocean while chasing the wind.

And though I'm frightened, I believe in your being with me. A man has to fend and fettle for the best, and then trust in something beyond himself. You can't insure against the future, except by really believing in the best bit of you, and in the power beyond it. So I believe in the little flame between us. For me now, it's the only thing in the world. - D.H. Lawrence

I am afraid when the time comes that I am already in love with someone else, you'll come again and I will still choose you, even if I know that you might hurt me again. It's funny how I used to argue with fate. How every night, I screamed to the heavens and asked them why did they have to keep us apart. I have always believed that you were my soulmate, that no matter what the circumstance is, we'd always find our way to each other. The universe told me we were just not meant to be and the heavens reasoned with me that I deserved better. The stars and the moon shone and said that someone out there was wishing and praying for my arrival but my heart constantly whispered it only wanted you.

I would love to tell you that everything will work out for us, and I promise to do all I can to make sure it does. But if we never meet again and this is truly goodbye, I know we will see each other again in another life. We will find each other again, and maybe the stars will have changed, and we will not only love each other in that time, but for all the times we've had before. - Nicholas Sparks

We look at each other beyond what the eyes can see, penetrating the soul. "That halo around your beautiful head had better just be the sun glinting off a pair of devil horns because I don't need a saviour, I need someone who'll burn with me." "I can't save you," she says. I say, "I just want a voice that's louder than my own." She looks at me so gently. She has eyes that make me want to cry. "I love you," she says, "to eternity and back. But there is no voice louder than the one inside your head. You have to save yourself from that."

I have found my star. She is beauty and grace. Elegance and goodness. My laughter in winter. She is courageous and strong. Bold and tempting. Unlike any other in all the universe, and I cannot touch her. I dare not even try. - Sherrilyn Kenyon

I'm amazed by her confidence and I often wonder where she gets all her strength. I love that she's happy in her own skin. That's something not to many women know how to be. There are often tiny moments where she is tentative, fragile and halting, but I always see those as her perfect little imperfections. Sometimes, I see myself in her. She is the fight in me, the winning and the losing battle. So therefore, I will dedicate myself to her imperfections, her uncertainty, her indecisiveness, her labours, her goals, her dreams and her passions. When they ask me who my favourite person is. I will say her. I will always say her.

But what I hope most of all is that you understand what I mean when I tell you that even though I do not know you, and even though I may never meet you, laugh with you, cry with you, or kiss you. I love you. With all my heart, I love you. - Alan Moore

Falling in love is not a choice. To stay in love is and we fall in love with someone for a reason. That reason is either temporary or permanent. When love leaves you. always remember no matter how broken you feel. bones mend, flowers grow back, scars heal, and one day you'll stumble across something that will make you feel whole again. No matter how lost you feel. Summer comes again, the leaves will change colour, the moon will reappear, the tide will settle back in, and one day the compass in your heart will point you back home.

When you're accustomed to loneliness, you become in tune with the rhythms of yourself and your own mind. You'll also know how important self-love and reliance is, to love yourself before you love someone else, but I think the universality of loneliness teaches us what that love is. To be lonely is to be human, to feel pain, to be forced to know yourself – and the universality of it binds us. Love is embracing that universality and surrendering to it. - Nico Lang

We were written across the universe into the very depths of every verse of every song. Through each line of prose and within each drop of sweet rain lay the whisper of you and I. The two who were one, bound by a love that was beyond comprehension and connected by one beautiful destination. You created this whole other world and I wondered how heaven could be any better. I held my breath, then laughed, convincing myself that maybe we had been soulmates in another lifetime but the world was not yet ready for our love story.

The whole time I was hoping my silence would fit yours and exclamation marks would gently float across time and space so that boundaries would be crossed; the whole time I was praying you would read my eyes and understand what I was never able to understand. - Anna Akhmatova

This long journey to your arms, this waiting in loneliness for the touch that awakens remnants of a life before, the kiss that ignites the dream of a thousand lives together, reunite as one in this embrace. Millions of years could not destroy this love, born time and again from darkness, our love unending, unyielding to time. This love is the multiplying universe, it is the creation and the divine, it is every fibre of life, every breath of every living thing born from the same spark of love, replicating itself in our single kiss.

All her life she had believed in something more, in the mystery that shape-shifted at the edge of her senses. It was the flutter of moth wings on glass and the promise of river nymphs in the dappled creek beds. It was the smell of oak trees on the summer evening she fell in love, and the way the dawn threw itself across the pond and turned the water to light. - Eowyn Ivey

Sometimes you may meet someone long after the time you have asked to, long after the time that you broke and when you realise that you may be chipped, you may be worn and dusty and broken in places but someone somewhere beyond the china cabinet is happy to piece you back together with soft, tender hands and nimble fingers despite the bruises that you bring and when he picked me up so gently by my handle, he told me that even the finest of china had cracks but only some see the beauty in repair and even less see the perfection in imperfection.

'You should always be happy.' He flattened his palm against the small of my back. 'I do not tell you often enough that I love you. I am not good with pretty words and flattery. But when I hold you in my arms, I feel as though I hold everything that is good and bright in the world.' - Jacqueline Carey

Words touch what the hands can't feel. The heart yearns for what the eyes can't see. The soul sings a melody that no ears can ever hear. The mind tastes the kisses that were never ever meant for the mouth. The air in our lungs travels further than our footsteps in one breath. How can you believe you are unremarkable when your very skin is enriched in miracles?

Tell me the word that will win you, and I will speak it. I will speak the stars of heaven into a crown for your head; I will speak the racing stream into a melody for your ears. I will speak the softness of night for your bed and the warmth of summer for your coverlet; I will speak the brightness of flame to light your way and the luster of gold to shine in your smile; I will speak until the hardness in you melts away and your heart is free. - Stephen R. Lawhead

She stood before me and suddenly I saw in her an interminable warmth and depth. A goodness untarnished by life's attempts. A love so pure and so true that nothing I said or did could break it. I just saw in her the strength I lacked, the light I sought, and the home I had never known. Her eyes quietly lifted and we stood together as still as the stars. I wanted to strum my fingers gently across her skin, like I was playing the slowest love song in the world and only she and I could hear it, but before I could, she opened her mouth and from her lips fell the song I'd been humming forever.

If we'd never met, I think I would have known my life wasn't complete. And I would have wandered the world in search of you, even if I didn't know who I was looking for. - Nicholas Sparks

She was the entire universe holding a billion galaxies in her heart. I remind her that the things that I love best about myself are the pieces of her, her softness, her forgiveness and her sacrifice. Her words were just like a cool evening breeze, like warm water on tired feet. The poetry on her lips puts my mind at ease. She gave me eyes when I couldn't see. I have learnt the world through her. She has taught me that there is no greater bravery than tenderness. I will carry her with me until I die, and when I do, whatever is left of me will shout her name into the heavens.

When they first kiss, there on the beach, they will kneel at the edge of the Pacific and say a prayer of thanks, sending all the stories of love inside them out in a fleet of bottles all across the oceans of the world. - Francesca Lia Block

We were moving into each other; I could now find a way home in the dark. When we first met, you were a beautiful disaster; a mystery that I'd hoped would remain as such. I was hopeful that the cloud of smoke would never clear, that you would stay veiled from me. But the mind yearns to decipher. It uproots veins and ripples at the sound of our beating entanglement. It aches to know. I was hopeful, hopeful that an ounce of my longing had taken refuge in your seclusion, as I've tried so hard to do. But I think love is geometric and will remain as such. You and I are parallel; no matter how close we get, we will never intersect. Our paths will never meet the way I have, and will always hope they might. No amount of hope could change the fate that had brought us so near. We're the brief moment of eye contact on two trains travelling in opposite directions but in a world full of moments, you were by far the most unforgettable.

I'm in love with you, and I know that love is just a shout into the void, and that oblivion is inevitable, and that we're all doomed and that there will come a day when all our labor has been returned to dust, and I know the sun will swallow the only earth we'll ever have, and I am in love with you. - John Green

I'm not searching for my other half because I'm not a half. I don't just want to be your sunshine; I want to be your full moon in a sky full of stars and the drops of rain that kiss your skin in the spring. I don't want to be sweet; I want to be your first bitter sip of coffee in the morning and like the metallic taste of blood when you bite the inside of your lip too hard and the salty taste of tears when you let yourself fall apart. I don't just want to give you butterflies; I want to give you intimate thoughts late at night and a memory so fond that when everything is over and all of this is done, you never feel, or taste, or love the same way ever again.

The heart has reasons that reason does not understand. - Blaise Pascal

Never ever leave someone who touches your soul more than your body. It is terrifying to think that one day you will trust somebody enough to let them see you naked. You will undress and remind them that you've got stretch marks and birthmarks and scars from having chicken pox when you were little and scars from all of the other things now. You will blush many thousands of shades of red, painting yourself as a rose losing its petals. And that person - that person will take it all in. And I wonder if they will reassure you. But mostly, I wonder if they will even see anything worth reassuring you about. I hope they see each freckle on your back as if it's a star and you are the whole universe to them.

I care not of the miles, the borders, or the oceans that may come between us. I will sail on the seas of your happiness, and I will travel across the perfect geography of your skin. I will study the constellations of your freckles and fill my life with the passport stamps from every corner of your body. I will explore you, and I swear on the breath you will steal, that not a soul on earth will find more to love. - Tyler Knott Gregso

You're like the sea. You're my worst nightmare yet so beautiful. I want to come home to you and taste the waiting on your lips. I want the roses in my hand to fall onto the floor because of the impact of your embrace. I want my nails etched into the trench of your back as you bury your head into my collarbone, while your lips unintentionally press against my neck. I want to feel the soft beating of your heart as it brings me to my knees. I want to taste the desire seeping through your skin and to hear the distress exhaled of your lungs. I want your sigh of relief and I want you endlessly. I want every inch of you as you've already taken me.

His love wasn't about looking back and loving something that would never change. It was about loving her for everything – for her brokenness and her fleeing. It was about touching that hair with the side of his fingertip, and knowing yet plumbing fearlessly the depths of her ocean eyes. - Alice Sebold

She's the type of person you'd write a book about. I would take the first three chapters to describe the way her touch sets my skin on fire. She loves it when I tell her that her voice sounds like earl grey tea and her laugh like manic pencil scratches; that I always draw out the pattern of her freckles on restaurant napkins; that she is the princess I told my little sister bedtime stories about; that her eyelashes look pretty when she cries and when I speak her name, my voice trembles like a violin string.

The female heart is a labyrinth of subtleties. If you really want to possess a woman, you must think like her, and the first thing to do is to win over her soul. The rest, that sweet, soft wrapping that steals away your senses and your virtue, is a bonus. - Carlos Ruiz Zafón

Every time I'm trying to move on people always ask me what I'm running from, but never thought to ask what I'm running to. I feel here is nothing wrong with closing doors that no longer even lead somewhere. I'm not the kind who searches for another source of warmth or comfort, to jump into the arms of another just to fill an empty space in my heart or to heal whatever's left. I just wouldn't do that to anyone. Am I so weak because I can't move on, or am I so strong, because I don't replace what's gone? Am I foolish because I have faith, or am I hopeful because I believe? Am I persistent because I keep trying or am I brave because I keep fighting? My intuitions, thoughts, feelings and what I know kill me because of their accuracy. We all know the right thing to do at times but deep down we find clues that tell us not to give up. It's delusional to convince myself every day that I'm over it when I'm not and to believe that there's a glimpse of hope. It's also contradictory of myself to tell myself I am happy when I feel so sad and I've read about strengths in letting go but I've also read about strengths in not giving up. What is the right thing to do? To fight for someone to be in your life or to let go and wait for miracles and fate to play their part? I can't go a day without thinking about you and if you ask me what's the point of all these words, it's simply everything.

This was a kind of dying. Losing the woman I truly had loved, and still loved more than anything, was just unfathomable. To me, she was the world. – Andres Lokko

You adore everything about him it's nothing that he does it's just him and these days, you often find yourself lying wide awake at night, wondering about the little things that he does. He makes you feel appreciated in more ways than one, and you love it. The very idea of him just playing with your hair. How he runs the softness of his hands on your skin, and the warmth of his palms running through your ribs as if he is washing away your every imperfection. The way he wraps his arms around your body, as he plants kisses on your lips, whispering to your ears words of endless forevers like soft melodies in a classic romantic movie. He breathes you in, and he embraces all your flaws, and how he never fails to remind you that you are beautiful. He's a million other things, and so much more. You want to plant kisses over his body so he'll grow to love himself as much as you love him; to drown his pain with love, and banish his loneliness with your affection. To only cause him tears of joy as you slowly rid him of his bitter past, creating memories that he can treasure. To simply want him in every way possible, to assure him that his battles will never again be fought alone, because you are here to love him, to care for him, and to support him now and for each day that follows.

Somewhere in the world there was a young woman with such splendid understanding that she'd see him entire, like a poem or story, and find his words so valuable that when he confessed his apprehensions she would explain why they were in fact the very things that made him precious to her. - John Barth

Far too often we value a body more than a soul. I look at you and I see something very magical, something so amazing that makes me fall for you over and over again. I look at you and see something so tempting that makes me want you even more and I look at you and see something that I can't be without. Sometimes you can't explain what you see in a person. It's just the way they take you to a place where no one else can. And of all the things my hands have held, the best by far is you.

She was like a forest, like the dark interlacing of the oakwood, humming inaudibly with a myriad of unfolding buds. Meanwhile the birds of desire were asleep in the vast interlaced intricacy of her body. - D.H. Lawrence

And how odd it is to be haunted by someone that is still alive. I don't know. I just feel stuck, like I'm afraid to take any steps in case they're the wrong ones.I wish you were in this room with me right now. I wish I could put my arms around you. I wish I could touch you. I hope you see my face in every passing car and hear my voice in your favourite songs and you realise I was the one all along. How can emptiness be so heavy? I think one of the saddest things is when two people really get to know each other well: their secrets, their fears, their favourite things, what they love, what they hate, literally everything, and then they go back to being strangers.

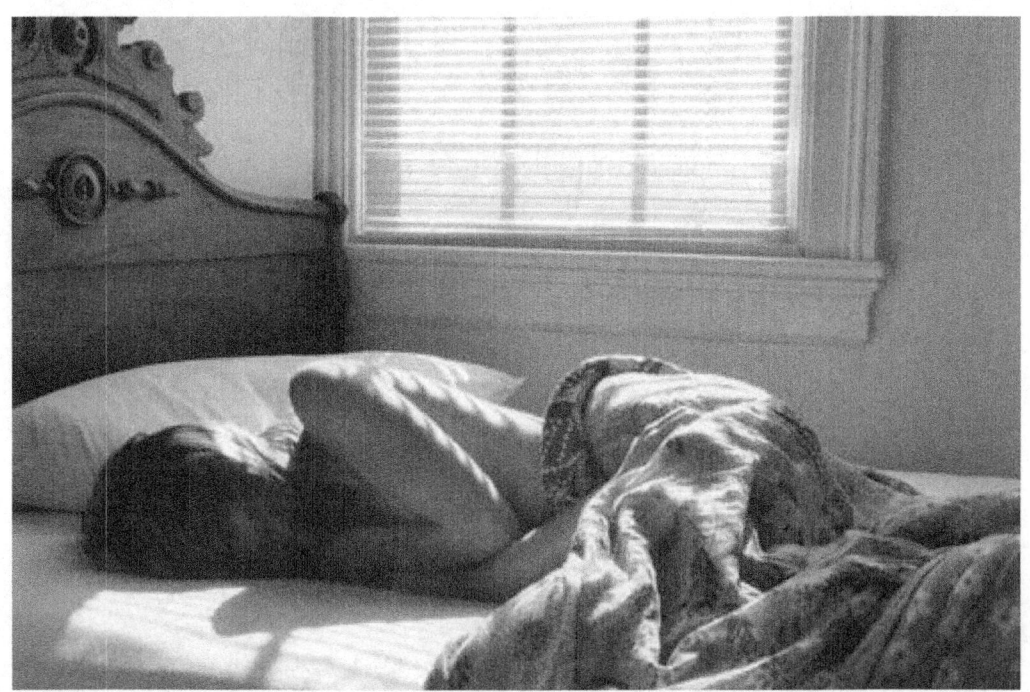

I guess by now I should know enough about loss to realize that you never really stop missing someone - you just learn to live around the huge gaping hole of their absence. - Alyson Noel

I am with her because I actually want to be with her, because I actually see a potential future with her, not because I am used to being with her, not because I am scared of the thought that being without her will ruin me. I look at her, and I'm home. There is no one else in this world that I feel both so comfortable and yet so nervous around, but still feel good about myself. Everyone is either one or the other, and I don't let people see me the way she does. She may have a dented halo and broken wings but that's the beauty about her.

The skies bend, the time stops, the lanes move and the fires dance, it can mean only one thing, that I am with you. You are enigmatic yet so beautiful that I have lost my sense, you are as immaculate as the unadulterated morning dew and your beauty leaves me in a mystified trance. I do not foresee what you and I will be, but I promise to be with you 'til the rocks keep meeting the sea. - Faraaz Kazi

When we very first met, you always refused to sing to me in public but whenever we would go for a walk, I always seemed to catch you quietly humming the sound of my heartbeat. Whenever you held my hand, I felt you very carefully forming the chorus of my veins. Whenever you held me, it's as if you were somehow connecting the bridge of my bones. And whenever you lay your head upon my chest, I knew that you were memorizing the rhythm of my heartstrings. You never overtly sang in public, but you still studied me as if I were an orchestrated symphony.

Please always know that behind all of my human behaviors, behind the best of me and the worst of me, behind the ego struggling to survive – is my soul, longing to mingle with yours. - Elizabeth Lesser

I simply have the greatest admiration for you. You have both the strength and grace of an archangel after everything that you have been through. You have taught me the true meaning of happiness. Your smile, the colour of your eyes, the way they dance and light up when you are truly happy about something, the sheer confidence and certainty of your words and actions, your evident faith in goodness and all beauty, your voice and yes, even your damned self-restraint are just a few of the reasons a moment with you is worth every heartache. You are entirely worth it. And perhaps in the end, I will have learned the practice of loving you well, loving you faithfully, and loving you greatly, regardless of the cost. Because in case I haven't told you lately, you are entirely worth it.

They say,' he whispers, his lips making the word-shapes on her shoulder, 'There is a river that heals all wounds. It is pure white, like snow or the blossoms of prarie-cotton. You are my white river. If I die, I will come back to wash my heart in you. - Margaret Lawrence

Words aren't enough to describe you. You are simply a man who means the universe to me. When I say I love you I don't just say it to hear you say it back. I say it because there cannot ever be a truer sentence that could be spoken. Your touch could only ever be described as magical as no matter where you put your fingers on me it could always make me shiver with need and anticipation. From a gentle stroke across my cheek to a pleasurable rub down my body. Every time you touched me, sparks flowed like electricity through my blood and made my heart sing. When you love a man, I mean really deeply love a man to the very depth of your soul, there is something so different about the way he touches you that mere words can not describe the feeling. Just being so near you made all my senses come alive. Yet your touch could enhance the senses tenfold. When your gentle hand reaches out for me, I can't stop my body from instinctively leaning in, drawn to your touch as if it is the only way I can truly ever be complete.

I can't tell you exactly what I'm looking for, but I'll know it when it happens. I want to be breathless and weak, crumpled by the entrance of another person inside my soul. - Aimee Bender

When the monsters of the night knock loudly at the gates of her mind, I will fill her with soft light illuminated from the sun that her eyes are incapable of seeing. And when the devils resist and continue their pursuit to whisper ugly words of sadness in her ears I will cover them to protect the evil from taking the innocence still living in her soul. And when she cries out of angst and self loathing I will press my lips upon hers to remind her that I am still here. And when she begs me not to leave I will hold onto her tiny body tighter in a mute promise that I will never abandon the secretive whispers that we share while bathing in the moonlight or the tender moments where our lips touch even for a second at the break of dawn. And when she says I love you, I will not take it for granted because I love her too.

He gripped her waist, tugged her closer to his chest and laughed that fortified, viscous sound. It slid over her skin in the same way his hand was gliding over her body. Every touch sending ripples out into a desolate past. - Elsa Holland

I want you to teach me the language of your bones. I have seen you peel back the curtain of your flesh from your ribcage enough times to know that you're wrong about your heart. You have got enough holes to last almost a lifetime but I have chained mine into my chest for all these years and yet yours is still somehow twice as whole as mine. So guide my hand along the curve of your spine and let me know just what it's like to feel as though you've got a place to rest your head and dream of home. I've simply been thinking of your lips for hours and it frightens me that I just can't seem to remember what your promise tasted like the night we knotted our limbs together and loved each other without making love. So whisper to me and be heard, a quiet heart speaks loud and though darkness hides its face, some certain truths still show. I want you to teach me the language of your skin. The first time we kissed, you dropped confessions into my palms that reminded me of the shoe box of unsent love letters kept hidden under my bed. I have read each one a thousand times but can never seem to fill the gaps in my lungs that formed each time you softly breathed my name. Sometimes, if I let the noise of the late night quiet tuck itself in bed beside me, I can almost feel your gentle fingertips entwined with mine. Behind my eyelids I see your sweet mouth pressing my favourite poem along my stomach and sometimes, I even manage to convince myself that I am fluent in the rhythm of your pulse whispering against my neck. I am found now in the arms of calm enduring, a love that knows no limit and no bound.

If you were mine, I'd lay you on silk sheets and wrap you up in ropes of pearls, and feed you honey from a silver spoon. Of course, you wouldn't be able to make all your high-minded judgements if you were a fallen woman but you wouldn't care. Because I would pleasure you every night, all night, until you forgot your own name. Until you were willing to do things that would shock you in the light of day. I would debauch you from your head down to your innocent little toes. - Lisa Kleypas

She has moved on and now I am repairing her broken heart. I feel sorry for you, because she overlooked your flaws, your temper, your selfishness, your inability to love anyone but yourself. She could have had anyone in the world, but she still chose you every time. All you are now is a crease in her past, a scar on her chest, a memory that fades faster than an old photograph of you in a sealed box, hidden. Maybe now she will fight for someone who loves her, instead of someone who sucks the life out of her. I hope you find little pieces of her in everyone you meet so she doesn't fade from your memory like wreckage sleeping at the bottom of the sea. And I hope you recognise her whisper in the way that they speak, a familiar echo resonating at some frequency so that you shiver when the nostalgia shoots down your spine, when your mind wanders back to those awkward, chaotic years so that you can never forget just how much you almost destroyed her.

Your absence has gone through me like a thread through a needle. Everything I do is stitched with its color.
- W. S. Merwin

So I reflect on the wonder of two lives, intertwined, two souls gently loving. Two hearts, wrapped in happiness. Not perfect. Yet perfect for each other. And perfect together with each other. And I pray to whatever deity that may be, that brought the blessing that is you into my life, that it may always be so. Touching my life with such gentleness. Bringing me a love so very powerful and a joy so intense, I never would have imagined it. Whose gentleness comforts me and whose smile brightens my day. Whose touch makes my soul sing. And I am so very happy. Simply content to bask in the warmth that is your love, knowing with certainty that to contribute to your joy would be my finest hour. My only wish is that we always continue to be joyful together. My only gift I really have to offer you is my unconditional heart. And the only gift I really want from you is to allow me to be by your side and hold your hand. Just a simple touch. A simple smile. A simple "I love you". These are the things my joy is made of. I love you so very much. Thank you for teaching me what that really means. Now I find myself no longer looking at the past, but rather to the days ahead with you by my side.

We are born to love as we are born to die, and in between the heartbeats of those two great mysteries, lies all the tangled undergrowth of our tiny lives. There is nowhere to go but through. And so we walk on, lost, and lost again in the mapless wilderness of love. - Tim Farrington

Hold me tight. Kiss me in the dark and press your lips against my neck. Breathe my name as you wrap your arms around my waist and pull me in. Trace the line of my hip up my side with fingers that tremble with desire. Wrap your fingers in my hair. Stand still and let me run my hands across your chest and feel your heart beat faster. All the poetry that is whispered in hushed tones on quiet corners, all the promises of a night like this, let it be done. No more words, simply speak to me in braille.

A wild angel had appeared to him, the angel of mortal youth and beauty, an envoy from the fair courts of life, to throw open before him in an instant of ecstasy the gates of all the ways of error and glory. - James Joyce

You come from nowhere and seduce my mind. Our conversations into the night, your voice a melody in my ear, singing to the very heart of me. Small talk will not hold me for long, I thirst to drink from your endless imagination and speak in the colours of your dreams. You talk to me in terms of the universe and I know that, from now, I will follow you anywhere.

I lived for half a century until wordlessly we met. I learn tonight how many years of learning by heart I waited for you. - John Berger

You call me crazy for saying that I'm in love with the very air that you breathe but I'm in love with every single component that contributes to the person you are. Every single detail about you reinforces the fact that they helped create a beautiful human being. And so the air, the air that so willingly travels throughout your body, encircling your body, keeping you alive. How could I be anything at all but in love? If only you see me when you look at me, and hear me when I speak, then the aura of my love would encapsulate the essence of your heart and echo throughout the universe for all eternity. You see my love, mere words are simply exhausted from my lips and have escaped my feeble mind. There remains nothing ever spoken or ever written to amply describe the song you sing to my soul.

In the first kingdom of the stars, everything is always half beautiful. In the second kingdom of the stars, there is only you. - Richard Brautigan

I am waking up with a soft smile on my face with the remnants of a dream fresh in my mind and the warmth of you still flowing through me, I can still feel your arms wrapped around me and the warmth of your body laying beside me. I open my eyes ever so slowly and snuggle into the pillow and look out at the fresh morning sunlight, I do wish you were actually here and I was hugging you instead of your picture.
Walking through each of my days smiling and laughing because of you, not getting to see you in person but feeling you with me in every moment, it is a feeling I'd never trade. Smirking a little over something you said or laughing right out loud, sharing each day together with you and yet thousands of miles apart, my long distance lover and my best friend. The hours I spend talking with you is the time I look forward to each day, you make my life so wonderfully complete and fill all the hollow places inside me, I never knew what it felt like to be whole before. Even though we fall asleep each night in separate beds in different cities, you are more real to me then anything else. I love you more than I have the words to say.

I didn't go to the moon, I went much further; for time is the longest distance between two places. - Tennessee Williams

Because of you my love, I can now be fully whom I am meant to be. There exist no fears or barriers. With you I will walk in love towards light, together moving upwards through new astonishing dimensions, festooned with flowers and angels. and innumerable other delights that are other worldly, visionary in nature. So who are you my sweet love? I am not quite sure but that I wish to lose myself totally and completely in your enchanting spell. I am yours with the purest love and my ever thankful joyful heart.

There are winds of destiny that flow where you least expect them. Sometimes they gust with the fury of a hurricane, sometimes they barely fan one's cheek. But the winds cannot be denied, bringing as they often do, a future that is impossible to ignore. - Nicholas Sparks

For years now I have let you go assuming you were content and satisfied as was I. Every now and then I would think of you, hoping that you'd found happiness, bliss and love as I did, never believing our paths would cross again, and that the thread to my soul would fade with time and distance. It seems that the universe or fate intervened and mitigated a reunion on our behalf, rekindling the cooling embers that lay below the ashes of our love that was denied. In a single moment of time, a touch too electric, a smile, too warm, sparks our twin flames to erupt, to dance with each other once again.

His heart danced upon her movements like a cork upon a tide. He heard what her eyes said to him from beneath their cowl and knew that in some dim past, whether in life or revery, he had heard their tale before. - James Joyce

So when you finally get to see him again, your love will fly back into your hands. You will easily forget about all those numerous endless weeks of imagining your fingertips on his skin. You will forget about all the awful withdrawals you experienced from not being able to feel his lips against your own. You will once again be able to look into the eyes of a man who knows you better than you know yourself. Enjoy him. Feel his heart beat beautifully against your fingertips. Indulge in the feelings he has saved just for you, nestled carefully into the muscles of his body, waiting for you to come home.

You are my heart as it beats within my chest, my soul as it moves through my mind. The breath in my body that so fascinates you is your essence pouring in and out of me as a wave that drowns me over and over again until I cannot breathe for wanting you. - Jacquelyn Frank

Your gentle voice's warmth is capable of mimicking bright sunlight. I could recognize it anywhere. It's that distinct tone and natural pitch that can only and will eternally be yours. An unintentional yet soft melody, intelligent and bright, simply iridescent in the aura of such everyday gloom. I yearn to fall asleep under the constellations you speak of and sink into a love, a love accentuated by only the soft glimmer of your tongue. You can break apart the universe, crack open the stars, and drink from the milky galaxies, and I will not stand here idle in awe, for I have discovered your radiance only ages before. My heart lies in wait within the garden of earthly delights, longing to unfold the myth of you and I.

Long since, the desert wind wiped away our footprints in the sand, but at every second of my existence, I remember what happened, and you still walk in my dreams and in my reality. - Paulo Coelho

Some have bibles and some go to church but I found heaven in you. I could recognize you by touch alone, by smell; I would know you blind, by the way your breaths came. You had been traded from person to person like a gold coin that has begun to lose its lustre and too many hard, rough fingers and not enough soft hands had handled your fine texture, but you were still priceless to me. The memories of you are like dried rose petals sealed between the pages of my heart, and if someone were to crack this fragile novel open, my love for you would flood the world a second time.

Nothing which we are to perceive in this world equals the power of your intense fragility; whose texture compels me with the color of its countries, rendering death and forever with each breathing. I do not know what it is about you that closes and opens; only something in me understands the voice of your eyes is deeper than all roses. - E. E. Cummings

I will never forget the day I first saw you. I had always kept my heart in a nearby drawer amongst all the unopened love letters and overdue bills. You were not an optical illusion, my eyes were not witnessing a mirage. Apparently it is realistically possible for someone to be so perfect as my heart and eyes both agreed on something for the very first time. Your photos were best compared to that of an exquisite painting, perfectly sketched by masterful hands. Attractive, breathtakingly attractive. Mere words fail to describe the beauty of this man as I lay there feeling besotted over some gorgeous soul I hardly even knew. There's no running back now as my beating heart lays imprisoned by life's cruel game of chance and bitter circumstance. I can only ever wish someone like you would one day be mine.

I can't sleep, I can't eat, I can't do anything but think about him. All night I dream of him, all day I want to see him, and when I do see him my heart turns over and I think I will faint with desire. - Phillipa Gregory

His love caused me to write the silliest sonnets about the colour of his eyes and the beauty of his smile. He was the best mistake that I had ever made. Or maybe it was the other way around because it felt as though I didn't deserve such love. I just didn't deserve to be loved in such an utmost unconditional way. I couldn't do anything in this world to earn the shelter he had offered me. He planted roses in my heart, lilies in my eyes and daisies on my lips and through his hard work, he never let a single flower die. He loved me through my darkest night and during my highest tides. He never left when my circumstances got the best of me. He never once left my side. Even when I didn't deserve it. He was my rock, my saviour, he was the love of my life. I would kiss the dimples off his cheeks and let him take the very light from my eyes if it meant only one more day of happiness together.

I would like to be the air that inhabits you, for a moment only. I would like to be that unnoticed and that necessary. - Margaret Atwood

For the ones who say my heart is cold, they are not false; you are the only one who has as yet found out the way to melt it. I had completely immersed myself into a world of my own making, until you opened my eyes to a new reality. A reality which is as alive and as tangible as the flowers in spring. In you, my wildest dreams bloom. Engrave your words upon my heart until their ink flows through my veins, fill me up with your stories, my love, and let me breathe again.

Perhaps the most important thing we bring to another person is the silence in us, not the sort of silence that is filled with unspoken criticism or hard withdrawal. The sort of silence that is a place of refuge, of rest, of acceptance of someone as they are. We are all hungry for this other silence. It is hard to find. In its presence we can remember something beyond the moment, a strength on which to build a life. Silence is a place of great power and healing. - Rachel Naomi Remen, M.D.

Sometimes I don't want words. I just want to close my eyes and feel at peace with the beat, the rhythm, my soul, the sadness in my heart. Like thunder the silence echoes in my head. Fear that my very heart beat will wake you as I watch you dream battles with my need to keep you safe as you sleep. My heart races with utter anticipation as my mind wonders at the joy you have shown me. You are beautiful. You are mine. You are my everything. My life began when you came to me, and my future is sleeping beside me. My breath catches as you stir, is this it? Is this the moment you awaken and my life resumes? For while you sleep I will protect you, and when you awaken I will live. Until then my darling, sweet dreams.

He knew that when he kissed this girl, and forever wed his unutterable visions to her perishable breath, his mind would never romp again like the mind of God. So he waited, listening for a moment longer to the tuning-fork that had been struck upon a star. Then he kissed her. At his lips' touch she blossomed for him like a flower and the incarnation was complete. - F. Scott Fitzgerald

When I first met him four years ago my heart was perpetually on vacation, stuffed between the pages of Austen and Murakami. He taught me to be braver, to be even that little bit stronger and when absolutely no-one was watching, he taught me that love could just absolutely destroy you. And he taught me to hold my heart, even if tiny pieces fell away, like it held all the secrets to simply being human; he looked at me with calm, soft eyes and kissed me and said 'when you're ready to fall again, make sure that I am here to catch you'.

And yet I adore him. I think he's quite crazy, and with no place or occupation in life, and far from happy, and philosophically irresponsible – and there is absolutely nobody like him. - Vladimir Nabokov

Every thought that I have begins and ends with you. I have aimed to write whispers of poetry, words silent enough to steal their way into your heart undetected. But your words were an open-mouthed kiss, a shouted love song to match my tender sonnet. I can't always craft my thoughts into such intricately woven stanzas like you do. Sometimes perhaps a tiny basket of broken fragments can express more than a well-worded composition. I feel that all I can offer is a plethora of undisciplined squeals of emotion. I'm not naive about us. I know that it won't be beautiful all the time but just trust me when I say I want the fire and I'm prepared to burn.

I think I fell in love with her, a little bit. Isn't that dumb? But it was like I knew her. Like she was my oldest, dearest friend. The kind of person you can tell anything to, no matter how bad, and they'll still love you, because they know you. I wanted to go with her. I wanted her to notice me. And then she stopped walking. Under the moon, she stopped. And looked at us. She looked at me. Maybe she was trying to tell me something; I don't know. She probably didn't even know I was there. But I'll always love her. All my life. - Neil Gaiman

As we lay together, I looked at his eyes and then looked up at the sky and I realized that both were just as extraordinarily blue as the other. With him I had begun to feel again, something that I have been carefully avoiding until this moment - because apathy is so much tidier than passion, and I was afraid to make a mess. He made me want to believe in life again made me want to sink my whole being into my existence instead of scrabbling uselessly against its surface. He made me think that there is hope in each morning and freedom in every night. When I'm with him, I think that I could begin to try again. In him I've found a kindred spirit, a kind soul. I've found in him a million sunrises and endless starry nights. I've found someone to believe in and someone who finally makes me believe in myself.

Falling in love with you was like coming to a place I didn't realize I'd been missing all my life. You're the only person I've ever known who accepts me for who I am, right in this moment, faults and all, and isn't waiting for me to become someone else. - Jennifer Chiaverini

He is a keeper for sure. His smiles are a lot like the lines from my favourite poetry. I just want to commit each one forever into my memory. He is someone who intrigues me beyond the point of comprehension. Someone who electrifies all of the very cells of my body, who ignites the surface of my skin when we touch. Someone who sees me more for my soul substance rather than the sum of my parts. He simply understands how to keep me, how to enliven even the darkest corners of my entire universe. He falls in love with me daily, with the subtle nuances that I have saved just for him. He knows what he has and what he could lose, what we would lose, together if ever we were to unravel and what we will gain by joining ourselves, by being near each other. And we will grow and deepen with our complexities and our vulnerable simplicity and continue to understand that the final chapter of our love will never be written.

It was the sort of bone deep emotion that made him want to hold her tighter with one hand, and draw a sword against the world with the other. - Jeaniene Frost

Meeting you was like listening to a song for the first time and just knowing that it would always be my most favourite. Before I met you, I felt a kind of homesickness for a place a certain je ne sais quoi that I did not even know existed. All it took was a kiss from your lips to take me there. It is you that reminds me of that place of familiarity that I have been longing for, a place I did not know, but deep down have always craved. Resting my head on your chest, hearing the dancing of your heart, home has never felt closer.

A couple of times in your life, it happens like that. You meet a stranger, and all you know is that you need to know everything about him. - Lisa Kleypas

He showed her all of his cards and decided to go all in with her, despite not knowing any of hers. He was weak to her touch, like clay in her hands, being gently and softly molded by her into a new man. Her touch was always very tender, smoothing out the imperfections that had been there for such a long time. Her soft voice gently whispering her affirmation and his senses attuned to hearing every syllable she spoke. So she showed him the tempest that raged within her, the strength of her heart, the stubborness of her will and the soul that burned like fire and he took all she had to offer, saw the beauty among the chaos, stared every flaw, every doubt and every fear in the face. All this, although he'd never felt more alive, simply left him completely breathless.

You came into my life, not as one comes to visit, but as one comes to a kingdom where all the rivers have been waiting for your reflection, all the roads, for your steps. - Vladimir Nabokov

I know her past is somewhat messy, a canvas of pain and deceit, I know it has shaped the person that she is today but she is deep in my soul, her lips are against mine and I can taste all her beautiful words. Our intimacy can be seen as the foreplay to everything life and a partner can offer you, so I now embrace the amazing ability to unleash every breath as I am spoiled by the most primal act. The two of us becoming one through our whispers, nouns and verbs performing in unison and ending in perfect harmony.

Yet everything that touches us, me and you, takes us together like a violin's bow, which draws one voice out of two separate strings. - Rainer Maria Rilke

How can I simply stay focused on anything but you, when your sweet poison so quietly pervades my mind? The totally inexplicable madness of you runs endlessly through my veins, the same way the rivers flow into the ocean. And it will be as so until the end of my time. Because I know that without you, I could never return to being the man I once was. If you are to leave, you must take me with you, for all you would leave behind would be an empty body left heartless, breathless and mindless. Only a love so pure could come over a man who would have otherwise never let anyone in to invade his being. But you have shown me that you mean no harm. And this poison never requires an antidote, for I will die happy with you running through my veins and the sound of the many "I love you's" we have whispered over the years resonating in my ears.

In your light I learn how to love. In your beauty, how to make poems. You dance inside my chest where no-one sees you, but sometimes I do, and that sight becomes this art. - Rumi

The pieces from your puzzle would never fit with anyone else's because they were meant for me. I had patiently waited and searched diligently and one simple hello changed the course of our lives. You were unsure if I would be your perfect match, so hesitant you were, until we began slowly putting all our broken pieces together one by one. Uniquely shaped by all the many different experiences we had from our past, we were both so unsure if this could truly be. Nonetheless we fitted together with ease and it finally feels good to have found our match. We no longer have the desire to fit in anywhere else than with each other.

And maybe one day, somewhere in between now and tomorrow, we can find our way back into each other's arms. Maybe then, we can finally understand what it feels like to come home. - Kelsey Gustafsson

Your smile is my poetry, your laughter is my song, your face is my story and your love is my everything. We never loved in nervous glances or in hopeful touches of our hands. We loved long before we noticed it in those late-night conversations about the universe and that casual, dependable interaction we never realized we would come to need so much. We loved in long talks about anything and everything, in brief hugs that started out just a little mundane but eventually came to be something more, leaving us with butterflies fluttering around our eyes and swirling happily about in our stomachs. We loved in walks in the forest and in adventures around town. We loved so slowly, yet increasingly, in a gradual, most beautiful kind of blossoming that left the world behind and brightened the stars in the sky. And it was that gentle love that drove us forward, softly illuminating each day and bathing us in a warm summer glow filling our lives with everlasting sunshine.

When I see you, the world stops. It stops and all that exists for me is you and my eyes staring at you. There's nothing else. No noise, no other people, no thoughts or worries, no yesterday, no tomorrow. The world just stops, and it is a beautiful place, and there is only you. Just you, and my eyes staring at you. - James Frey

They were both made of dust from the same star. She loved him, and when you love someone, even their so called flaws become beautiful. She traced his scars with careful fingertips ' I want you to know that I love your flaws'. He pushed her hand away and quietly whispered ' they aren't flaws, they are just little signposts to where I've been '. She had never ever wanted something safe. She had always wanted something of a storm with raging feelings and hands that couldn't keep away from each other. She wanted spontaneous visits and their two bodies intertwined. She simply wanted to make sure she treated him right. She just wanted to fight for him and care for him and he in return gave her something that made her very insides combust with what felt like a universe exploding in her.

From the moment I first saw him - saw through his stunning and impossibly gorgeous exterior to the dark and dangerous man inside - I'd felt the pull that came from finding the other half of myself. I needed him like I needed my heart to beat, and he'd put himself in great jeopardy, risking everything - for me. - Sylvia Day

I do not know where lost things go, but I swear to keep your name tucked beneath my tongue so all my words would know the shape of you just the same way rivers know their stones and I didn't ever get to write you down because I was afraid my pen wouldn't let you go, my paper would swallow you whole. I was always taught to hold on to a beautiful thing. So, no, my fingers will never unfold from the spaces in your soul. My footprints will never ever point towards the door. My name will never ever be a past tense shattered on your floor. You are a beautiful that steals away breaths. The kind I can't help but keep all to myself.

I kept your name buried deep inside, and when I had nothing else to cling to, with a single whisper in the dark I would name you, careful not to be heard, and in doing so, something of you would be restored to me, and something of myself would be saved. - Peter Hobbs

The warmth that I have searched my whole life for, was found within your arms. The peace and happiness of me finally feeling truly at home. I found that one winter night, in the form of your bright blue eyes and in your soft welcoming smile. A sparkle that was just made for only me. I simply saw everything I wanted to be in your eyes that night. You devoured me a like flame set upon kerosene. Your tongue was magic and well placed between soft nibbles. You were my every desire. I wanted more. I needed you to taste my lust feeding the warmth that was rising within me. My whole body vibrated craving the taboo. I wished to be in the room again, another me somehow watching you touch me in a way no man ever had. I wanted to be able to rewind our moments to the first time you made me shudder as you fingers ran along my thigh. And I wanted to never forget this moment. A smile escaped my lips that only you could bring. And years later the fire that was lit, has grown brighter than the sun. The warmth you bring to me lightens my very soul Though distance may come between us at times, it is in your arms, I know that I'm finally home.

She didn't want soft and gentle. She needed his rough possession, claiming her, branding her, taking her in a firestorm of heat and flame that would end the world around them, leaving them nothing but ashes, clean and fierce and forever welded together. - Christine Feehan

Your gentle voice has a depth in which I could dissolve and just sit totally breathless, your haunting melody encircling my body, drowning me in the deepest pools of desire. You approach me softly, gather my hair carefully in your hand, sweep it slowly aside, and brush your soft warm lips against the geography of my neck and shoulder. I love the delicate delicious way in which my name slides from your tongue, simply flowing into passionate pools of melody, waning whispers to stifled screams each time my name passes your lips and I swear that I can taste you. Listening to your words as they glide into my ears, the gentle atmosphere permeating my skin and warming the inner depths of the frozen areas of my soul. It is like spoken music. It is like poetry. Your quiet song has summoned the shadows, they bleed across the walls in a phantom waltz to soften the very sadness of my solitude It is like breathing oxygen for the very first time or being dead and being revived. It is an awakening of my soul.

Real intimacy is a sacred experience. It never exposes its secret trust and belonging to the voyeuristic eye of a neon culture. Real intimacy is of the soul, and the soul is reserved. - John O'Donohue

Maybe I fall in love too easily but after him I didn't think getting up was ever an option again. After him I was supposed to stay down, settled among the ground, content with the leaves and earth. I fell for security but there was nothing secure about the dark emptiness that consumed me every time he disappeared and left me alone in the moon's silver light. So maybe I do fall in love too easily but you came with your arms, picked me up and showed me that falling isn't quite so permanent and just how else would broken hearts become mended if previously shattered souls never shared their healing song…

The way to love someone is to lightly run your finger over that person's soul until you find a crack, and then gently pour your love into that crack. - Keith Miller .

She kissed me, no she gave me her breath. Perhaps that's not right either, because she took my breath away. I inhaled her and yet she took the air from my lungs. She stole my soul, except she gave me new life. But more than this, much more that this. I finally knew what it meant to be kissed. She was my very conscious. She saw into my heart and soul and accepted it as it was meant to be. She could see things as they came, touched people where they needed to heal and all at her own expense. She was not of this world. Something that fell from space, flaming like a star not meant for a mere mortal such as myself.

Because if you're lucky enough to have people in your life that make you happy, that inspire you, that move you, you need to devour each moment you have together because you never know how many of those moments you have left. These people are sacred. - Katie Kacvinsky

Haunting the deepest tunnels of their minds they came forth to each other. She was a child of the night, born to look up at the night skies. To stare at stars and feel them staring back, to watch the moon wax and wane and to feel her soul howl, but yet say nothing. Yes, she was cut from a cloth of many, but she was her own person, and she found peace in the stars. He was born with constellations in his eyes, an entire universe within his soul, too big for one small planet, lost among the crowd of blank stares, but isolated just the same. When she saw him, she knew she had finally found her chance to be among the stars and when he saw her, he felt seen. She had always wondered how such a big world could fit inside one body and he wondered why she was so different from the rest. She had always felt small while watching the skies, but looking at him, she felt even smaller. He was so much more than she had ever seen before. He wasn't just the part of the sky she could see, he was the whole thing. He was nothing like the rest. A whole planet full of people made of grey, but he shone with colours she didn't even know existed. She had always dreamed of catching a shooting star in a glass so she could always have a piece of the sky. But instead, the whole sky fell down in the form of a man, who held her and whispered "I love you".

I have for the first time found what I can truly love - I have found you. You are my sympathy - my better self - my good angel - I am bound to you with a strong attachment. I think you good, gifted, lovely: a fervent, a solemn passion is conceived in my heart; it leans to you, draws you to my centre and spring of life, wrap my existence about you - and, kindling in pure, powerful flame, fuses you and me in one. - Charlotte Brontë

I will make you an angel of my music. Your very presence could illuminate a whole room, blindingly. How you caress away all the crevices darkness hides and bring darkness to absolution, simply softly reminding it how it has allowed for the depth, the meaning in life, but also simultaneously reminding it that it can come and play in the light for a while and bask in your good intentions. I want to taste the beauty inside your soul, to dip my tongue into its quiet streams, scrape my teeth gently across your love, touch my soft lips to the smoothness of our forever. I can feel a storm brewing, your heart overflowing, your soul in need of release, a scream building deep inside and I have often warned you that this might happen. I have told you that the fever would come, the rush would be powerful, intoxicating you. I have told you that you will always be safe, I will hold you so close, our bonds will be strong enough to weather the storm, with every stray breath and whisper, with the heart that floats and the roots that anchor me, with every atom and all of the spaces in between them. I will love you.

I want to see you. Know your voice. Recognize you when you first come 'round the corner. Sense your scent when I come into a room you've just left. Know the lift of your heel, the glide of your foot. Become familiar with the way you purse your lips then let them part, just the slightest bit, when I lean in to your space and kiss you. I want to know the joy of how you whisper "more". - Rumi

Sometimes the only thing to do is release yourself into the physicality of the moment. Feel all that your body has to show you and just dissolve into the moment, live within the perfect sensation of the present. Maybe someday I will write something worthy of your skin, because you have painted your portrait on this porcelain heart and you've sewn your verses into my soul, making me whole. And for that short time, while you hold me, I feel a great freedom fill my heart, a quiet calm comes to both my body and soul and a smile soars to my face. I have found my home. There is no time here the clock has stopped. This is not simply a moment but a lifetime. No it does not end here, there is more than this, this is my forever at your feet.

To get the full value of joy you must have someone to divide it with. - Mark Twain

Please handle me with care and remember always to open me slowly. My pages have been tattered and worn by the careless readers of yesterday. Treat me with care, like an old tome. Read me with your soft gentle fingers tracing every word, letting them reverberate and echo within you. Feel the sound of my words as they tickle your tongue, sing like a symphony as I tell my story. Please don't ever grow bored with my rambling, my purple prose and my awkward sentences, my comma splices, and my run-ons and the many chapters that interrupt my complete thoughts and run into each other and seem to never end or begin with a sense of time or meaning. I ask that you accept all my inconsistencies, all my contradictions. I am not well-researched, but I am written from the heart. And I want you to read me and to take your time with me, learning every word by rote, even though it may turn repetitive and drag sometimes. Still there will always be something new there, something hiding in the margin, some uncovered feeling if you remove the dust that is layered on my pages. But please, always remember that I am extremely fragile so open me slowly and handle me with care.

It's beautiful when you find someone that is in love with your mind. Someone that wants to undress your conscience and make love to your thoughts. Someone that wants to watch you slowly take down all the walls you've built up around your mind and let them inside. - Unknown

Your touch could only be described as magical. I never knew it would feel like embers on my skin as your hands moved over every soft curve or how your breath would move across the swell of my chest every single time you pushed into my heart, my body. No matter where you put your fingers on me it could always make me shiver with need and anticipation. Every time you touched me, sparks flowed like electricity through my blood and made my heart sing. When I never knew what it was like to feel you, I never ached for you before, not like I do now. Then I could miss you. I could long to close the distance between us but I never knew what it was to have you. I suddenly understood what it would be like for you to live here inside of me but the aching abyss of your absence is the only thing reminding me I didn't dream up the whole damn thing. There is a hole in the shape of you lying next to me in bed every night and some days the gap seems endless miles on miles on miles. I want to build bridges out of my words because maybe they will touch you before the next time my hands will. I am never where you are, but you are always with me and sometimes when I look at the moon, I can feel the pull of you. Your love is the only tide I've ever moved with.

There is one secret place, it is beautiful and peaceful, where gentle water flows, and a most beautiful garden grows, yet, nobody could ever go to. You reach deep within my soul drawing out all the dreams that I hid beneath the doubt for long casting all my feelings away into the darkness and shutting all the doors. Only, somehow, they were traced and found by you. - Oksana Rus

Well we should never ever underestimate the power of the caring touch, the tentative fingertips of our very first love. The so soft subtle grazing of fingertips on our face. I guess that if we were to ever think seriously about it and even to judge the very single most important of all of our five senses, to overlook the sense of feeling, of that gentle touch, would prove to be a very foolish oversight. A man could meet thousands of incredible women. He could see hundreds of them naked. He could taste dozens of them on his lips. But there just comes a time for every man when a woman enters his life that makes it hard for him to breathe whenever he sees her. When he becomes weak in the knees from her gentle touch. When a simple kiss makes him forget his name. That's when he finally realizes that the search is over.

A woman's heart should be so hidden in God that a man has to seek Him just to find her. - Max Lucado

So they would sit and talk for hours, these most unlikely of friends not caring that they were different, how it started or if it would end. They just revelled in each other and lived in the other's heart, these two unlikely companions who would be friends for life, never to part. As brick by brick her walls came down, letting in the light and sun, each languid kiss gave her a shot of scintillating pain; and he, smiling continued all the same, for he was a moth, and she, such a pretty, flickering flame. And so her body opened too, and her mind and her heart and soul, and words just came pouring, tumbling out. And they found safety, a safe haven in him. Even the unspoken ones were brave and scrambled to his shore. She had finally found her shelter in him.

I have a million things to talk to you about. All I want in this world is you. I want to see you and talk. I want the two of us to begin everything from the beginning. - Haruki Murakami

He turned towards the voice and searched for her scent. It felt natural, it felt right, there in the half light of the quiet room where there was only him, her, and no pretence, no defences needed or wanted, just a gift, given freely without thought, without the subtle nagging doubts or the sagging spirits that total surrender usually brings. Just a freedom of a body given, of a mind offered of a soul simply set free and in that very moment, that particular precise particle of space and time, she became his and, by doing so, entirely came into her own.

I'm not frightened. I'm not frightened of anything. The more I suffer, the more I love. Danger will only increase my love. It will sharpen it, forgive its vice. I will be the only angel you need. You will leave life even more beautiful than you entered it. Heaven will take you back and look at you and say: Only one thing can make a soul complete and that thing is love. - Bernard Schlink

My eyes saw the simple graceful line of her form, her soft symmetry, her defiant pose, even from bended knees; therefore, she was beautiful. My ears heard the hoarse whisper of her every need, bleeding through spoken words, words that I had barely heard; therefore, she was mine. My lips brushed with the force of a feather's touch at the trembling nape of her naked, outstretched neck; therefore, I existed. And when finally we kissed for the first time, she put her lips on my lips, and when she breathed it was like she was filling up a space in my being that had always been empty. With each subsequent exhalation, she gave to me a part of herself, while taking part of me in return, and no matter how far away we would end up from each other, I would always breathe the same air that she breathed, not knowing, or caring that I would never be able to breathe on my own again.

You only need one man to love you. But him to love you free like a wildfire, crazy like the moon, always like tomorrow, sudden like an inhale and overcoming like the tides. Only one man and all of this. - C. JoyBell C.

My love for you is simple, a gentle gathering of quiet emotions, a passing of tangled butterflies playing in the breeze. It is not burdened with a freight train full of fantasies, just the comfortable tune of wind, and leaves, and fireplaces, and thoughts of you. My fingers are ships sailing on your skin, slowly drifting and hoping against hope that they just fall off the edge of the earth. And your heart is nothing but gravity pulling me towards you. One day, our ribcages and our souls will burst softly open and then the truth of who we all really are will float out of our hearts and our heads. And you and I, we will truly see each other. Perhaps for the very first time.

There is a primal reassurance in being touched, in knowing that someone else, someone close to you, wants to be touching you. There is a bone-deep security that goes with the brush of a human hand, a silent, reflex-level affirmation that someone is near, that someone cares. - Jim Butcher

She has her unique fractures along her heart, and you have yours. And maybe there is nothing, anywhere, that doesn't break someone's heart. Never ever seek to take by force, those things only reached in silence. Never seek to rule the day, when the day will come to you. Never rage in hope of winning, the prize awaits a gentle touch. Look not to subjugate the willing, such give greatly as they are. Use your open hands to call her, wait and know the end is sure. All her dreams have but one refuge; in you they must reside. Time will teach her love, love will teach her pain and in the end, time will teach her to love again.

There is freedom waiting for you, on the breezes of the sky, and you ask "What if I fall?" Oh but my darling, what if you fly? - Erin Hanson

I will always be left to wander and chase the shadows of the glimmering girl, never to hear your voice again but always to hold instead the hand of your memory, real only for those brief moments before you ran. And I know that one day someone will love you. For me, love is both an emotion and an action, like light is both a particle and a wave. Someone will love you like light moves through glass, just as if their sunlight could shatter windows and shine on the shadows, in your heart. To the right person, you will be so much more than enough. To the right person, you will certainly never be looked upon as a compromise; a settlement. You will become their very dream embodied; the unexpected answer to wordless questions asked in the middle of countless long, lonely nights. To the right person, you will become the most precious thing this life has to offer; the reason for life itself and when they uncork the jar holding your hopes, you will feel a soft fluttering like the wings of a bird, and suddenly your dreams will again take flight.

Someone can be madly in love with you and still not be ready. They can love you in a way you have never been loved and still not join you on the bridge. And whatever their reasons you must leave. Because you never ever have to inspire anyone to meet you on the bridge. You never ever have to convince someone to do the work to be ready. There is more extraordinary love, more love that you have never seen, out here in this wide and wild universe. And there is the love that will be ready. - Nayyirah Waheed

I gave you my lips for a moment but your kiss made me yours for life. Your lips are the whispers of dreams long since evanesced with the smoke of snuffed out birthday candles. The light weight of your soft fingers skimming my exposed back is the repressed pressure of your distant glances, where I shiver at the graze of your eyes over my body like a ghost of emotion. Your voice, deep throaty, constricted by desire, hums in my ear displaying that I am not the only one with overflowing ventricles and lightning stormed synapses. Your gentle hands give me dopamine goosebumps across my skin. I sigh into you, wanting only to be the parasitic vine that climbs upon your oaken structure, intertwined for all eternity.

Mysteries of attraction could not always be explained through logic. Sometimes the fractures in two separate souls became the very hinges that held them together. - Lisa Kleypas

"I am just a little lonely," she whispered ."Come and hold me for a while." So he took her in his arms. "Pain's not easy and neither is healing. You just let the past go. It has no meaning. You've been hurt and you're still not free. Break free of your chains, leave it all behind and come be broken with me." And when the sun stretched its long rays and waved goodbye to the moon an eternity later, it could no longer even distinguish, in the tangled haze, which limbs were his and which were hers. And then she realised that the journey was the destination and what she had been looking for was inside her all along.

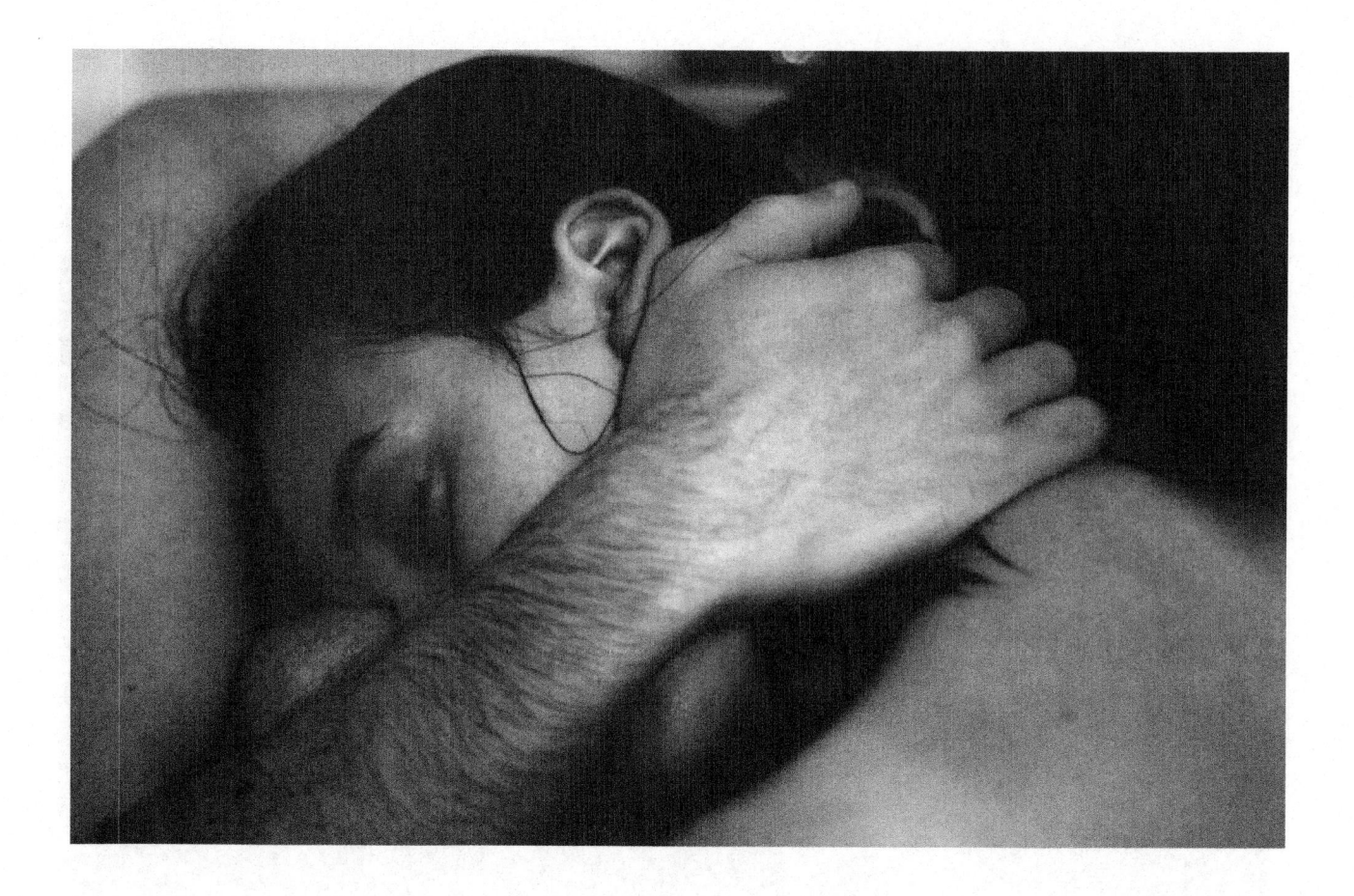

All she ever wanted was unpredictable kisses and unforgettable laughter. - Brandon Villasenor

Sometimes it is for all the world to see, but only for two to truly understand. Passion is a disregard for balance; for safety; for stifling stability. It blooms within the dim unknown, the place the mind can't see, blossoming in the vacuous void where all our inhibitions have been destroyed. Passion is a willingness to build our hopes upon the softest sand; the jumping, falling forward, never knowing where, or how, or if we'll land. Such passion as I'd never felt, it swept me up, embraced me, ignited in me new and yet untold flames, kept unknown fires raging, like liquid entering through my skin, and finding a home within.

Those who love you are not fooled by mistakes you have made or dark images you hold about yourself. They remember your beauty when you feel ugly; your wholeness when you are broken; your innocence when you feel guilty; and your purpose when you are confused. - Alan H. Cohen

There's a map beneath her soft skin and all her veins are rivers, there are directions and instructions written in secret on her bones, there's a star he cannot see that shines in a north he will never know. And there's a secret current, beneath the waves, that carries him to the end of her. He knows every road, every hill and valley and every channel. And when he travels her world with expert tread, he creates entirely new lakes and oceans. Fallen from the pedestal that she had constructed for herself, she found herself leaning on his. Strengthened by his assurance that it would always be there, she went to seek slightly more comfortable dwellings but she returned time and again, to touch the cold marble, study its hard edges, and found such beauty and warmth in the steadfast, even stone. In time he quietly lifted her to him, and she became his 'Eternal Springtime' to her 'Kiss', her graceful curves resting against his strong and unwavering marble for eternity.

The ties that bind us are sometimes impossible to explain. They connect us, even after it seems like the ties should be broken. Some bonds defy distance, and time, and logic. Because some ties are simply meant to be. - Meredith Grey

It is through the shadows we travel to see our truest selves, to see our brightest lights. There was a light you gave me. "Keep it safe," you said, "as I will keep you." No matter where you take me, your hand guides me to somewhere I've not been before, a road less travelled, somewhere where rules of old need not apply and where my naked soul resides. Can you feel the air between us? Do you sense the goosebumps on my skin as your hand approaches? Do you feel the tremble in my limbs, do you hear my tender heart leap ever so briefly? And as your hand reaches my skin, do you feel the sigh in my soul, the way I melt into your touch? And each word you whisper in my ear adds to the goosebumps your fingers have found. If there is any air left, I cannot find it, simply because you leave me breathless. Some parts of the body cannot lie even if you want them to. It is in the brightest light that I am most thankful to share your shadows.

Some people bring out the worst in you, others bring out the best, and then there are those remarkably rare, addictive ones who just bring out the most. Of everything. They make you feel so alive that you'd follow them straight into hell, just to keep getting your fix. - Karen Marie Moning

Imagine meeting someone who understands even the dustiest corners of your mixed-up soul. What is the point of travelling to hell if you are going to take the safest road? Find the one with the hairpin turns along steep jagged cliffs. The one that will not just only rattle your teeth, but your very soul. The one that has milestones in the middle of it that you have to veer to miss. The one that has signposts pointing in every direction but up. The point of the journey is to live. And if that journey ends in a hail of brimstone and fire sparks, as long as you were true to yourself and loved with your whole heart, then who is to say that the journey was not worth it. Life is to be lived. To thine own self be true. The rest is just icing. So hold the fire in your hand to feed the hunger, raise the stakes or quench its thirst, suffocate it and the slightest breath is all the fuel it will need to fan the flames of unbridled passion.

I have a secret. You can build walls all the way to the sky and I will find a way to fly above them. You can try to pin me down with a hundred thousand arms, but I will find a way to resist. And there are many of us out there, more than you think. People who refuse to stop believing. People who refuse to come to earth. People who love in a world without walls, people who love into hate, into refusal, against hope,and without fear. I love you. Remember. They cannot take it. - Lauren Oliver.

Sometimes, a single, cherished memory is the only thing powerful enough to get you through to the one yet to come. A moment in time as fleeting as the wings of a butterfly. As searing as the hottest flames. As long lasting as the memory of your soft voice as you whispered my name. As beautiful as a warm green meadow. As deep as the ocean blue. As large as the smile I hope to wear when I pause to think of you. The first tiny flutter happened when your eyes met mine. The wings went faster the minute you smiled. And when you touched me a million butterflies all took flight inside every inch of me. I lived for that moment...

Passion. It lies in all of us. Sleeping... waiting... and though unwanted, unbidden, it will stir... open its jaws and howl. It speaks to us... guides us. Passion rules us all. And we obey. What other choice do we have? Passion is the source of our finest moments. The joy of love... the clarity of hatred... the ecstasy of grief. It hurts sometimes more than we can bear. If we could live without passion, maybe we'd know some kind of peace. But we would be hollow. Empty rooms, shuttered and dank. Without passion, we'd be truly dead. - Joss Whedon

It's the way you touch, claiming skin, bones, muscle and sinew with your soft gentle hands, the way your voice enters me, draws me out, makes me float. It's the way you breathe life into me, the way your hands, your fingers, your breath simply melt me, powerless to resist. My heart opens to your voice like the flowers open to the kisses of the dawn. It's simply the way I am, yours. So I will dress my heart and mind in what I love, I will always fill my eyes with wonder and chase the things that inspire and delight me, for with you, is where I live.

Sometimes your nearness takes my breath away; and all the things I want to say can find no voice. Then, in silence, I can only hope my eyes will speak my heart. - Robert Sext

You speak to me softly talking of our love. You describe the way I touch the back of your neck at 1am wondering how I have managed to live a lifetime in the span of a few years and how when it rains I always think the sky is crying for some lost soul that hasn't yet found a home. I couldn't tell you where my wounds begin, if my scars are really all that noticeable. All I know is that your love has managed simply to keep my demons at bay despite their almost constant howling and all I ask is that you lean into my fingers and not flinch when I kiss your collarbones. We are all ghosts darling, don't you see? I am here waning like a moon and yet you're here shining glorious as the sun. Where I am the darkness, you are my light.

When two people really connect, something is poured out of one and into the other that has the power to heal the soul of its deepest wounds and restore it to health. The one who receives, experiences the joy of being healed. And the one who gives, knows even greater joy of being used to heal. - Larry Crabb

Even if she writes down everything that's ever crossed her heart, there will still come a day when none of her words can explain how she feels. At first glance she appears strong. At first glance she appears most determined. At first glance her world is quiet and she is calm. At first glance she appears to be waiting, but only at first glance. If you really looked at her. If you really saw her, you would see she is very fragile. You would see she is vulnerable. You would see the chaos inside her. You would see her, but you have to get past your first glance. And then to find eyes to see her for what she is, hands to comfort, arms to protect and the heart and mind to tame the chaos within.

One of the deepest feminine pleasures is when a man stands full, present, and unreactive in the midst of his woman's emotional storms. When he stays present with her, and loves her through the layers of wildness and closure, then she feels his trustability, and she can relax. - David Deida

She spoke words that warmed his soul and calmed his heart. He could feel her warmth and softness as he approached. Her scent, that sweet scent of her body flooding the room. Her eyes a mix of dreamy soulful lust and fiery intense passion. He very gently took her soft hand, and he lead her through the darkness, not because she was weak, but because she was weary of being strong; not because she was helpless, but because she yearned for his help, and he so longed to give it; not because she was just lost in the silken shroud of the ebony night, but because he was lost, and in leading her, he found a light within himself to guide their way. They spoke not a word as they fell into an embrace. But it was more than that, they simply reached each other's souls. Darkness eclipsing the light, as the whole of the world broke away. They bled into each other, the way lovers do.

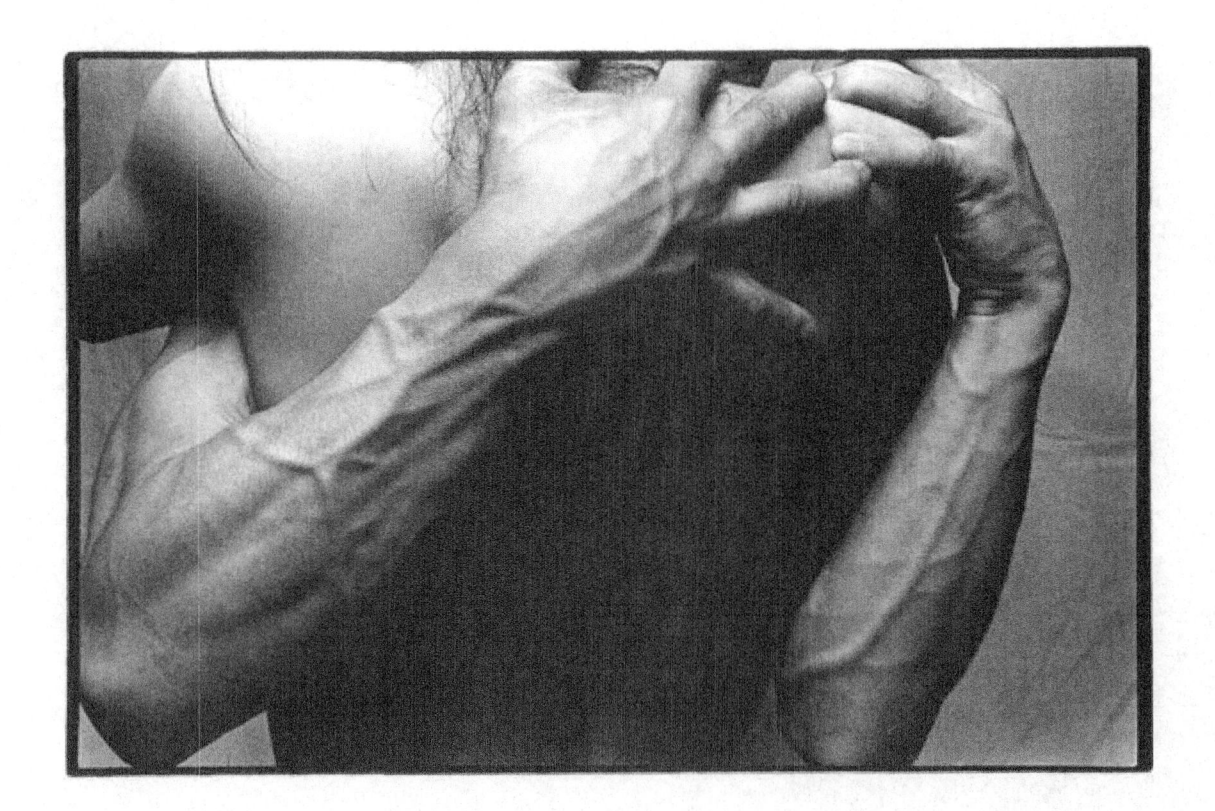

You must learn her. You must know the reason why she is silent. You must trace her weakest spots. You must write to her. You must remind her that you are there. You must know how long it takes for her to give up. You must be there to hold her when she is about to. You must love her because many have tried and failed. And she wants to know that she is worthy to be loved, that she is worthy to be kept. - Junot Díaz

She knew if she was lucky, one day she'd get the chance to have her life truly defined by how much she loved and was loved by someone else. The fractures and fissures of her time worn heart caused her to see the world with cracks and crevices. Most would see that as broken, battered and yet she still was naive enough to see butterfly wings through stained bubble glass. It never mattered whether he wanted her or not, she belonged to him outright the moment she showed him her brokenness and he kept looking at her like she was whole. Despite her turbulent past she possessed the strength and the intellect, the inherent worth to intimidate, to dominate nearly the whole of humanity. Yet, she searched for the one who would not buckle beneath her strength; who would not be at all intimidated by her own mental prowess; who would not hide his eyes from the brilliant light that she exuded, the one to whom she might bow without a flicker of shame in her heart.

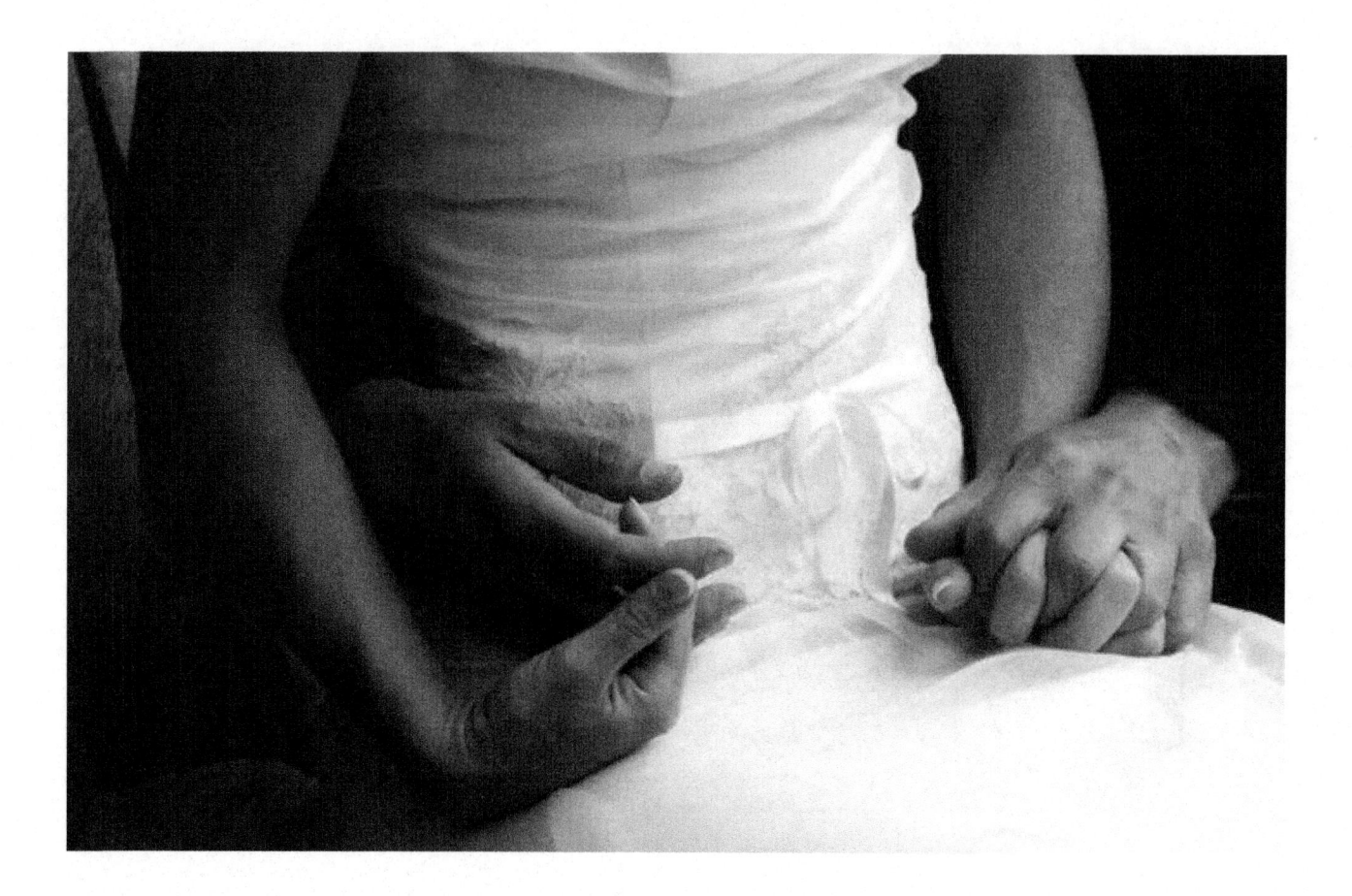

Most people assume that a muse is a creature of perfect beauty, poise and grace. Like the creatures from Greek mythology. They're wrong. In fact, there should be a marked absence of perfection in a muse - a gaping hole between what she is and what she might be. The ideal muse is a woman whose rough edges and contradictions drive you to fill in the blanks of her character. She is the irritant to your creativity. A remarkable possibility, waiting to be formed. - Kathleen Tessaro

Even in the darkness she shines so brilliantly. I could say that her body is poetry, but that would be a massive understatement. Her body is scripture. Her body is meant to be perused over and over, to be revered and never understood. Her body is simply divine. Scripture, and really the only fitting reaction, worship. I could also say that her body is a song, an enchanting conception of sweet melancholy, but this too would be an understatement. Her body is a symphony. Her body is an awakening rhythm and deafening beauty. Her body is not a choice, it is a compulsion, a song that demands a dance and I could also say that she is my true great obsession, but that would not just be an understatement, it would be a lie. She is a need, a longing, an ache from a hollow emptiness that will not be dismissed. I long to see her begin, so slowly, so reticent, fighting through hesitance, a timid shiver of wind, stirring soon to a breeze; to watch her as she lets go, as she twirls and she spins with peace born of a new found release; but I know, as I have known all along, I cannot ever force her to dance. I just merely give her my song.

I chose you, not because I think it will always be easy, but because with you I know that even on the dreadful, wretched, luckless days, when the troubles of the world are downpours of thick, clamouring, beating rain - you will laugh, take my hand, and whisper delightfully, dance with me. - Beau Christopher Taplin

Find us on Facebook at
https://www.facebook.com/Visions-Of-Love-1467308783508714



Follow us on Twitter at https://twitter.com/JaneWil46902663



We also have a website http://visionsoflove.co.uk/



Copyright 2015

Printed in Great Britain
by Amazon